Let This Be The Year

by

Chloë Mitchell

Let This Be The Year
by
Chloë Mitchell

Book Cover by Ashley Newman

No part of this publication may be
reproduced, distributed, or transmitted in any
form or by any means, including
photocopying, recording, or other electronic
or mechanical methods, without the prior
written permission of the author.

ISBN: 9781724190017

To those who are and are not.

-Chloë Mitchell

Let This Be The Year

365 Daily Meditations

1

Make the commitment to commit to yourself.

2

Understand that the love you give won't always be the love returned.

3

Master the art of shutting people out who
do not bring you positivity.

4

Love yourself unconditionally and without restrictions.

5

Get shit done.

No more excuses.

6

Let go of feeling angry and bitter towards someone.

Anger only turns your heart cold and poisons you from the inside out.

7

Accept that some people are temporary
seat fillers in your life.

8

No longer will you force people to stay in your life when they start to distance themselves.

9

Stop taking everything personal.

10

Drop the dead weight.

Happiness is so much lighter to carry.

11

Learn to mind your business and yours alone.

12

Sometimes saying "no" to others is saying "yes" to yourself.

13

No one knows how hard you work[ed].

It's ok to applaud yourself.
Be proud of you.

14

Whoever and whatever is important to you, let it be known.

15

Start believing in yourself.

Give yourself pep talks.
Be your own hype man.

16

It's ok not to be ok.

17

A bump in the road isn't the end of the road.

Keep going.

18

Your happiness is a top priority.

19

Giving attention to your past stunts your mental growth.

20

Trust yourself.

Know that what you have to offer is worth
the risk.

21

Don't overthink it.

22

Always have more than one option.

LET THIS BE THE YEAR

23

Know your worth.

Those close to you should always
lift you up
Inspire you
motivate you
and most importantly, love you.

24

Always be willing to make necessary changes in your life, not only when a new year is approaching.

25

Give people space.

Sometimes we must give others space to find themselves, even if it hurts us as a result.

26

Never settle for mediocre love again.

You aren't mediocre.
You're extraordinary.

27

Don't ask for apologies.

If someone owes you one, you should
never have to ask for it.
Either their ego is too big or they aren't
sorry.

28

You won't be liked by everyone, no matter how hard you try.

29

Love is about patience and the willingness
to love without stipulations.

30

Pray for clarity and a sound

mind
body
and spirit.

31

Be selective of the type of energy you
surround yourself with.

The energy you keep around can effect the
energy within.

32

Stop entertaining what or who you don't like.

33

Stop explaining yourself to others.

Don't waste too much time proving yourself.

34

Do not accept half truths as honesty.

People should be completely honest or
say nothing at all.

35

When you settle, you are negotiating what you deserve.

What you deserve is not up for debate.

36

Let go of convenient relationships.

There is nothing worse than being a ghost
in someone's phone.

37

Keep your standards high and your faith
higher.

38

Open your heart to

forgiveness
happiness
blessings
positivity
and love.

39

Emancipate yourself from

pain
stress
drama
negativity
and heartbreak.

40

Do not be afraid of confrontation.

It is one of the most uncomfortable situations to be in, but feeling used and bullied is even more unsettling.

41

Acknowledge people's faulty patterns with you.

They are well aware of their change in behavior towards you.

42

When you lose trust in others, find trust in God.

43

Build yourself up.

Don't let people or things build on you.

44

Pray when you lose the answers.

Pray when you find them.

45

Remind yourself who you are and what
your purpose is.

Sometimes we lose sight of what our goals
and achievements are.
Never stop reminding yourself.

46

Your love is a privilege.

Not everyone is deserving of your love
and it's ok to be stingy with it.

47

If you would never destroy yourself, why would you give others the power to do it for you?

48

Time heals nothing but prayer heals
everything in time.

49

Give yourself and others emotional
support.

We are not built to go through things
completely alone.
Sometimes, you may have to but when
you don't have to, don't.

50

Don't allow people to take advantage of
your emotional availability.

51

Everyone's path is different.

Seek your own path.
Create your own path.
Mind your own path.
Believe in your own path.
Nurture your own path.
Own your own path.

52

Protect your heart.

Don't give it to just anyone.

53

Inhale and exhale.

Take a moment to just breathe and feel
your lungs expand and contract.

54

Embrace the change that is occurring in your life.

We may not always be ready for what is to come, but change is inevitable and necessary.

55

Fear hinders you from being great.

56

Respect is not restricted to age, but to maturity as well.

57

Pray for everything.

Pray on everything.

58

A failed relationship is by no means the death of love.

There will be plenty of opportunities to get it right.

59

The absence of romantic love is not the absence of love in it's entirety.

60

Treat yourself and those you love all year round, not only for special occasions.

61

Find someone who will pray for you and with you.

62

Let go of those who take advantage of your love.

Stop holding on to dead love.

LET THIS BE THE YEAR

63

Start something new.

64

Sometimes it may take an entire year to see that some of the relationships you have aren't healthy ones.

65

The value you have for yourself is the value you have for others.

How you treat others is a reflection of you. How you allow others to treat you is also a reflection of you.

66

Chances expire.

People always deserve a few chances to clean up their messes and right their wrongs, but never be a doormat for anyones love or friendship.

67

Stop convincing yourself that you owe someone your presence.

If it does not benefit you for the betterment of your heart and spirit, the only thing you have to give is your absence.

68

Show and then tell.

Always let your work speak for itself.

69

Mental stimulation is one of the first
qualities you look for in a partner.

70

The quality of friends is more important than the quantity of friends you think you need.

71

Travel to a place you've never been to.

72

Learn the value of patience.

Nothing happens when you want it to happen, only when it is meant to.

73

Stand up for

someone
something
or yourself.

74

Stop responding to those text messages
and phone calls.

75

You may be the root to your own problems.

76

Time is non-refundable.

77

Stop complaining and find solutions to
your issues.

78

No one is obligated to you, even if they make a promise.

79

Just go for it.

Don't go through life with
I wish
I should've
If only
moments.

80

Stop being afraid.

Be afraid of
not trying
not knowing
and having regrets.

81

Put all of your energy into you.

82

Don't get discouraged.

LET THIS BE THE YEAR

83

Stay true to yourself.

84

Teach people how to treat you.

85

Pay attention to the signs.

They are always around you, you're just
blinded by the circumstances.

86

Don't let anyone disrupt your inner peace.

87

Get rid of every toxic entity that's
poisoning your life.

88

Like the weather, situations and people are seasonal too.

89

Whoever wants to be with you, will be with you without hesitation or excuses.

90

If someone cares, you'll know.

If they don't care, you'll know.

91

Get rid of those who treat you as if you are easily replaceable.

92

Make sure your actions always match your words.

No one ever signs up for half the effort.

93

It's ok to need a pair of hands to hold you
and those same hands to pray for you.

94

The healing process begins the moment you accept that you are hurting.

95

Hold yourself accountable.

96

Stop getting territorial over who does not belong to you.

97

Some people are not equipped to give
you what you ask for.

98

In the end, always do it for you.

99

Allow people to be their true selves.

You can either accept them 100% or not at all.

100

You will fall in love again.

101

Never become complacent with where you
are in life.

Always strive for more.

102

Understand that those you once rooted for, won't always be the same ones rooting for you.

103

Stop letting people turn you against
yourself.

It is a tactic used by those who see your
power as well as your vulnerability.

104

Stay up to watch the sun rise and fall
asleep to the moon kissing your face.

105

Donate

your time
your intelligence
and your wisdom.

106

Be authentically you.

107

Say exactly what you want and don't want.

108

Your smile is your best accessory.

109

This won't be your last heartbreak but
don't let it jade you.

110

Say yes to what scares you.

111

If you don't know the answer, make the effort to do some research.

112

Let your passion destroy you in every beautiful way imaginable.

113

Defend the ones you love when they are not present to defend themselves.

114

Keep the promises you've made to yourself.

115

No longer will you surround yourself with people who drain your energy.

116

You deserve to be loved astronomically.

117

Let that negative energy go.

118

Stop letting people take advantage of you.

119

Meditate.

Being able to control your thoughts and
bring a calmness to yourself is imperative
to revitalization and restoration.

120

Physical
mental
emotional
abuse is not a form of love.

It is a form of manipulation and
psychological damage.

121

Believe that the love you're praying for is obtainable and that patience is the first step in achieving it.

122

Stop sleeping in on your dreams.

It is never too late to start anything, but why prolong something that could be done in the now?

123

Don't dumb yourself down to appeal to
someone else's idea of you.

124

Keep those complaints to yourself.

Depending on the circumstance, no one
wants to hear you complain all day.
Stop harping on it and let it go.

125

Work hard and work smart.

126

Ask for guidance.

You don't know it all, so stop presuming
that you do.

127

Stop looking for the one in everyone.

Everyone you date won't have the potential to be a life long partner.

128

Be humble but always be aware of your talent.

129

Don't let anyone make you feel
incompetent for anything in life.

130

Take criticism with grace.

131

Start over.

132

What is for you, will always be for you.

133

Find the lesson in everything.

134

Don't take yourself too seriously.

135

Getting to know someone will make for deeper understanding of the other person.

Take your time.

LET THIS BE THE YEAR

136

Check your email more than social media.

137

Spend more time engaging in face to face interactions.

138

Get yourself a mentor.

139

Listen carefully before you jump to a conclusion.

140

Keep a journal.

141

Fear births courage.

142

Mistakes are just the prequel to turning a scribble into a masterpiece.

143

Don't spread yourself thin.

144

Look at how far you're going instead of being distracted with how far you have to go.

145

Do not give in and allow someone a piece of you if they're not willing to take all of you.

Partial love is selfish and you deserve to be loved entirely.

146

Some arguments are pointless.

147

Revel in your solitude.

148

You are not a puppet.

Be an individual.

149

You are your greatest accomplishment.

150

50/50 is no longer the standard in relationships.

Both persons should be giving 100% in effort.

151

Growth is progress.

152

Challenge yourself in areas where you are not strong.

153

Being a winner is not someone who has succeeded, but someone who never saw failure in losing.

154

Practice productivity.

155

Adversity teaches you tenacity.

156

Pamper yourself.

157

Always make time for self reflection.

158

Embrace your flaws.

159

Know the difference between someone being nosey and someone who is actually concerned.

160

Don't let anyone disrespect you.

No one gets a pass.

161

Loving others is no easy feat.

Everyone has different love needs specific to them.

162

Don't let the idea of achieving perfection slow down your process of getting the work done.

163

Hold on for just a moment longer.

164

Be generous with the intent of nothing to
be gained but a happy heart.

165

Hold someone tight.

166

Allow someone to sit in silence with you
when all the words have left you.

167

Create your team.

Nothing great can be accomplished all on your own.

168

Don't discredit other work to make yours
appear better.

169

It is not love that is difficult, but the people in which you are dealing with.

170

Let things happen unscripted.

Not everything will be planned and it's ok
to go off course.

171

Let love seep in on places that were only filled with resentment.

172

It's ok to look silly.

173

Listen to your intuition, your gut feeling.

It will never steer you wrong.

174

Just because it feels good, doesn't mean it's good for you.

175

Become a person of compassion.

176

Get there early.

177

Admit that your mom/dad was right about that one thing.

178

Whatever you're praying for, make sure you're also praying for the wisdom to receive it properly once it is given.

179

Be sincere when you tell someone that you love them.

LET THIS BE THE YEAR

180

Don't feel guilty for taking a day off.

LET THIS BE THE YEAR

181

Pray for others well being.

182

Give praise to someone.

Everyone needs a little reassurance.

183

Be thorough and consistent.

184

Don't confuse missing someone's presence
with missing how they made you feel.

185

Keep your focus on those you love and
those who love you in return.

186

Be willing to do for yourself what others refuse to do.

187

Forgive yourself.

You can never move forward and live fully
if you keep beating yourself up over
something that happened in the past.

188

Don't get stuck liking someone who shows
no interest in you.

There's playing hard to get and then
there's not interested.

189

Call that person.

No one wants to write an essay about how their day went.

LET THIS BE THE YEAR

190

Don't wait on anyone.

191

Kindness is so attractive.

192

Home is not in places, but in people and experiences.

193

Don't allow yourself to feel lonely in the presence of others.

194

Chivalry is not dead.

You just haven't found that person who
feels you're worth the gesture.

195

Pain is just a tunnel through happiness, if you are willing to get to the other side.

196

Not giving a response is a response.

197

The slightest doubt can lead you to believe that you have failed before you have even started.

198

Someone else's bad day is not your bad day.

199

People won't always live up to the
expectations you have of them.

200

Let your heart heal from a breakup.

Don't jump into another situation or
relationship so soon.
Give yourself the space you need.

LET THIS BE THE YEAR

201

Wake up leaving any feelings of
inadequacy in yesterday.

202

Another day means another chance to get it right.

203

Stop making excuses for other people's wrong doings.

204

Maturity is best served in how you present yourself to others and most importantly, to yourself.

205

You are no one's second choice.

206

Create healthy habits.

207

Give yourself deadlines.

Nothing can truly be accomplished if you don't have a time frame in which you want things to be done.

208

Control and manage your anger.

209

Moderation replaces deprivation.

210

Don't measure your success by anyone else's.

211

You will not be able to control everything.

212

Separate what you want to do from what you need to do.

LET THIS BE THE YEAR

213

Your heart is always in it.

214

When you forgive, it is no longer collateral in the future.

215

Your
mental
sexual
spiritual
and physical health are all aligned.

216

With experience comes wisdom.

LET THIS BE THE YEAR

217

The advice you give to others is the same
advice you would follow.

218

Nothing new and exciting happens in a comfort zone.

219

You don't always have to have your guard up.

It's ok to be vulnerable.

220

Those who have nothing to lose will do all they can to see you lose all that you have gained.

221

Take a shower not only to cleanse your body but to cleanse your mind as well.

222

There is nothing wrong with being picky.

223

Show more gratitude than ungratefulness.

LET THIS BE THE YEAR

224

Accept that you won't always make the
best decisions.

225

Don't let anger get the best of you.

226

There is always better coming your way.

227

Manifest the things you want out of life.

228

Dream.
Plan.
Execute.

229

Do not rush into anything that requires forced energy.

230

Procrastination is the restraint that keeps you stagnant.

231

Save room for love that will be
reciprocated.

LET THIS BE THE YEAR

232

Adversity is your weapon.

233

Failure doesn't mean to give up, it means
to try it again differently.

234

Your only competition is the person staring back in your reflection.

235

Get enough sleep.

236

When you value your personal space, you'll be more inclined to be selective on who is able to enter it.

There should be restrictions on who has access to you.

237

Meaningless relationships and friendships, unsatisfying jobs and living situations must fall to the wayside.

238

Thank those for trusting you with their feelings.

239

Set boundaries.

240

Let the tears fall loudly and your hands
hold your face gently.

241

Don't say 'it's ok' when it isn't.

242

Kindness goes a long way.

243

Follow your heart but remember to use
logic.

244

You aren't always right.

245

It's ok to date yourself.

246

You are where you want to be.

247

Some people you'll grow with and others you'll grow from.

248

Whoever you drunk dial won't be a regret story.

249

You're no longer caught in a tornado.

250

Surrender to your stubbornness.

251

When your heart sinks with mourning, let
their love keep you afloat.

252

Stop seeking closure.

LET THIS BE THE YEAR

253

Drink more water.

254

It's ok to go from loving someone to having love for someone.

255

Stop pretending you're stronger than your emotions.

Nothing will humble you quicker than shedding some tears.

256

Keep some things to yourself.

257

Don't allow others to darken your light.

258

It's a hard thing to hear that you aren't
doing a good job at being the best person
from someone you love.

Be better. Do better.

259

It's ok to walk away.

260

Always do your best to help others but do not take ownership of something that does not belong to you.

261

Stop pouring yourself into others when it isn't being reciprocated.

Don't forget that you too are a flower that needs watering.

LET THIS BE THE YEAR

262

Your sanity is priceless.

263

Allow love to ignite a quiet riot inside of you.

264

Pretending a person no longer exists just to keep them out of your thoughts.

265

Fearlessness and ambition come with no apology.

LET THIS BE THE YEAR

266

Even if you are available, don't always be
available.

267

Stop holding on to a love that only benefits you.

Don't be selfish and deny someone the right to be loved by someone who can love them back.

268

Give someone flowers.

269

Celebrate the small victories too.

LET THIS BE THE YEAR

270

No more pity parties.

271

You can't fix everyone.

272

Being a product of your environment has a positive connotation.

273

Stop wasting your time on someone who treats your text messages like email.

274

Keep good company.

275

Staying in was a better idea.

276

Your gift is no longer a thing that collects dust.

277

It's ok to be the only one.

278

Be spontaneous.

279

Have an open mind.

280

Give a sincere apology.

281

Words can give people the power to feel
everything, as well as feel nothing.

282

Opportunity lies in the ones who are willing to try anything once.

283

Communication.
Mindfulness.
Understanding.
Listening.
Patience.
Honesty.
Respect.

Keys to a thriving relationship/friendship.

284

You can not expect a drama free life if everyone brings baggage.

LET THIS BE THE YEAR

285

Stop looking for validation.

You are not a ticket.

286

Wake up early to listen to the dewy silence
that stirs in your cup.

287

Stop feeling obligated to smile at someone who tells you to.

288

Don't be so hard on yourself.

289

Nothing is wrong with you if you're the only one in your friend group who isn't in a relationship.

290

If you feel uncomfortable about it, don't follow through on it.

291

The only pressure you feel is from
someone's lips against your own.

292

Go on a trip by yourself.

293

Worrying leads to stress leads to overthinking leads to problems that don't truly exist.

LET THIS BE THE YEAR

294

Respect vs. Likeness.

295

No one deserves unlimited opportunities
to hurt you.

296

Some people must be loved from afar.

LET THIS BE THE YEAR

297

Find peace within yourself.

298

Keep your hands warm in someone else's.

299

Being too prideful will leave you with just that.

LET THIS BE THE YEAR

300

Be present.

301

Ask for help.

302

It's ok to avoid people you don't want to "catch up" with.

303

Your tolerance for nonsense decreases.

304

It is a privilege to be invited into your space.

305

What is important to you will not always be important to everyone else.

306

Positive thinking is positive action is positive being.

307

Yelling won't make people hear you any clearer.

308

Appreciation is a verb.

309

Don't gravitate towards the one who seems confused about your position in their life.

310

Talk to someone.

LET THIS BE THE YEAR

311

Save your money.

312

Everyone won't make the cut for this year.

313

Your free time still costs you something.

314

A soulmate is not restricted to romantic relationships.

LET THIS BE THE YEAR

315

Stop wasting your own time.

316

Your energy is aligned to receive the blessings God has in store for you.

317

Let your tears of laughter be greater than your tears of pain.

LET THIS BE THE YEAR

318

Buy yourself flowers.

LET THIS BE THE YEAR

319

Never stop evolving.

320

Remain faithful during your journey.

LET THIS BE THE YEAR

321

Read more literature.

LET THIS BE THE YEAR

322

Loving yourself is a prerequisite for loving others.

323

The same dedication you put into someone else's company or business is the same worth ethic you need to have for your own.

324

The most successful people are the ones who didn't give up at the first time they heard 'no'.

325

In life, as you get older, you'll know the difference between the one who says they'll be there for you and the one who will be there with you.

326

Love without fear.

327

The sky is only the limit if you see those clouds as the ceiling.

328

Invest in your home.

Make it a space you never want to leave
and the place you can't wait to get to.

329

I love you.

The end or beginning of something beautiful.

330

Be thankful for the things you asked for
and didn't get.

331

You are the sun in someone's darkness.

332

When searching for a partner, you should already be the person you are seeking.

LET THIS BE THE YEAR

333

Always be prepared.

334

Finally get comfortable in your skin.

335

You are your own muse.

336

The definition of you is written by you and only you.

337

You too have toxic traits you need to work on.

338

There is comfort in silence.

LET THIS BE THE YEAR

339

Hold a high value for your privacy.

340

Write someone a letter.

341

Be with someone who makes you feel like magic.

342

Without effort, nothing can be accomplished.

343

Get lost in love with someone, but never
lose yourself in them.

344

You will be misunderstood at times but it is not your job to always make them understand.

345

Say the words you wish were said to you.

346

No longer will you apologize for being an introvert/extrovert.

347

Action precedes words.

348

Pain only seems permanent when you
refuse to let it go.

349

Respect and love are not synonymous.

350

Stop picking yourself apart.

351

Stop talking down on yourself.

Change the voice inside your head. Don't allow your thoughts to turn you against yourself.

352

Stop making excuses for someone who always has them.

353

When you put all of your energy, focus,
and attention on yourself, you
unintentionally create a barrier that blocks
anything that throws you off your course.

354

Just because they love you, doesn't mean
they know how to love you.

355

Beware of professional liars.

356

Appreciate being hurt from the truth than from a lie.

357

You can't and won't win them all.

358

Let go of whatever has been weighing you down.

359

Subtract yourself from what does not add to you.

360

Sometimes you have to fall apart to rebuild a better version of yourself.

361

Saying no doesn't always have to be followed with an explanation.

362

Sometimes you just need to fall back and disappear.

363

Return to yourself.

The love you have for yourself is your
antidote.

364

Love, be love, and allow to be loved.

LET THIS BE THE YEAR

365

Make this year the year you've been
looking forward to.

Ch

Instagram: @iamchloemitchell

Twitter: @imchloemitchell

imchloemitchell.tumblr.com

www.iamchloemitchell.com

Made in the USA
Monee, IL
21 January 2021